Marie-Claire Di Carlo

Mother Mary's Apparitions

AF889929

Marie-Claire Di Carlo

Mother Mary's Apparitions

From around the world

Blessed Hope Publishing

Imprint
Any brand names and product names mentioned in this book are subject to trademark, brand or patent protection and are trademarks or registered trademarks of their respective holders. The use of brand names, product names, common names, trade names, product descriptions etc. even without a particular marking in this work is in no way to be construed to mean that such names may be regarded as unrestricted in respect of trademark and brand protection legislation and could thus be used by anyone.

Cover image: www.ingimage.com

Publisher:
Blessed Hope Publishing
is a trademark of
International Book Market Service Ltd., member of OmniScriptum Publishing Group
17 Meldrum Street, Beau Bassin 71504, Mauritius

Printed at: see last page
ISBN: 978-613-7-88389-1

Copyright © Marie-Claire Di Carlo
Copyright © 2019 International Book Market Service Ltd., member of OmniScriptum Publishing Group

Our Lady, Help of Christians, Czech Republic

The feast day is on May 24th, my nephew Michael Di Carlo's birthday. May she always protect him.

On January 13, 1866 at 4 in the morning the Virgin appeared to a sickbed Magdalena Kade. She was miraculously cured from her long illness. Our Lady appeared dressed in white and with a golden tiara. A basilica was then constructed on the site and many miracles have occurred there.

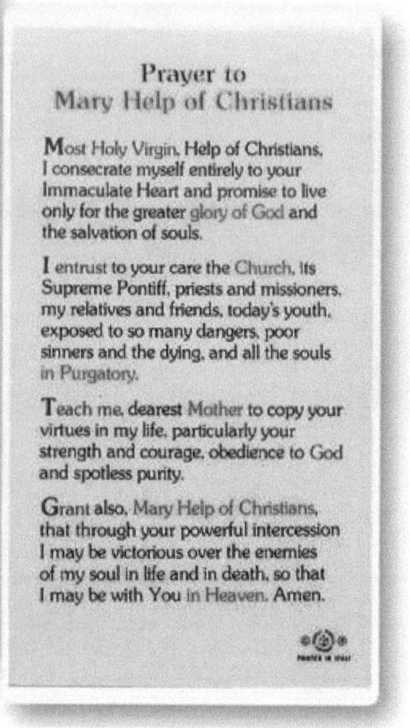

Prayer to Mary Help of Christians

Most Holy Virgin, Help of Christians, I consecrate myself entirely to your Immaculate Heart and promise to live only for the greater glory of God and the salvation of souls.

I entrust to your care the Church, its Supreme Pontiff, priests and missioners, my relatives and friends, today's youth, exposed to so many dangers, poor sinners and the dying, and all the souls in Purgatory.

Teach me, dearest Mother to copy your virtues in my life, particularly your strength and courage, obedience to God and spotless purity.

Grant also, Mary Help of Christians, that through your powerful intercession I may be victorious over the enemies of my soul in life and in death, so that I may be with You in Heaven. Amen.

Our Virgin's Birthday, Feast Day

My nephew, Ismael Di Carlo, is born on her feast day. I'm sure she protects him in many ways.

Happy
Birthday
Holy Mary, Mother of God pray for us sinners now and at the hour of our death.Amen
September 8

Our Lady of Mercy

Our Lady of Mercy's feast day is on September 24th and she is the patron saint of prisoners. She is my mother's saint since my mom's middle name is Mercedes. It was 1203 and the Muslims were taking captives of Christians and bringing them to Africa. A merchant by the name of Peter Nolasco tried his best by giving his money to buy the slaves and free them. He freed 300 captives, then he ran out of money and he prayed to God for help. The night of August 1 to 2 1218, the Blessed Virgin Mary appeared to him. She also appears to Raimundo de Penafort, and to King James I of Aragon and told them to help Peter make a congregation for the captives and to keep freeing the captives from the Muslims. When it was built their order took a fourth vow, chastity, obedience, charity and to dedicate their lives to freeing the slaves. Their first location was the hospital St. Eulalia. On one of Peter's expedition to Africa to free the slaves he became a prisoner and was able to free himself. Peter died at 77 years old.

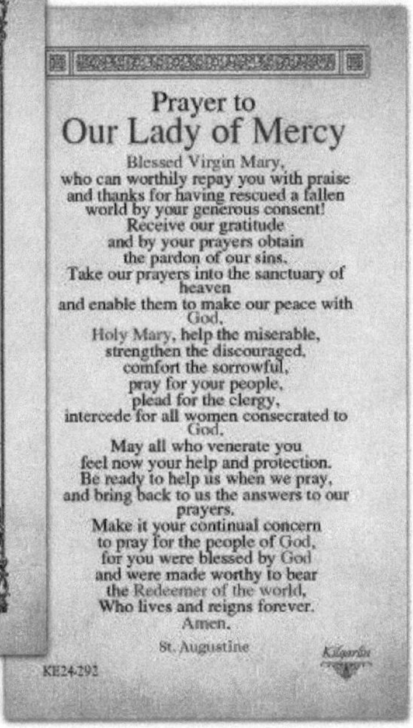

Prayer to
Our Lady of Mercy

Blessed Virgin Mary,
who can worthily repay you with praise
and thanks for having rescued a fallen
world by your generous consent!
Receive our gratitude
and by your prayers obtain
the pardon of our sins.
Take our prayers into the sanctuary of
heaven
and enable them to make our peace with
God.
Holy Mary, help the miserable,
strengthen the discouraged,
comfort the sorrowful,
pray for your people,
plead for the clergy,
intercede for all women consecrated to
God.
May all who venerate you
feel now your help and protection.
Be ready to help us when we pray,
and bring back to us the answers to our
prayers.
Make it your continual concern
to pray for the people of God,
for you were blessed by God
and were made worthy to bear
the Redeemer of the world,
Who lives and reigns forever.
Amen.

St. Augustine

KE24-292

Our Lady of Coromoto

My mother is from Venezuela and she loves our Lady of Coromoto, which was made the Patroness of Venezuela on May 1, 1942. When the city of Guanare was being founded in 1651 by Roman Catholics there was a tribe that already inhabited it and were resisting. La Virgen appeared to the chief of priests to be baptized near a river and he refused and then on Septemeber 8, 1652 she appeared in his hut and he tried to grab her but she vanished and left behind a painting of herself. In Guanare today there is a church dedicated to Our lady of Coromoto that was made into a national shrine on January 7, 1996.

Oración a la Virgen de Coromoto

¡Oh Santísima Virgen de Coromoto!, Madre de Diós y Madre nuestra, que escogiste a la nación Venezolana para manifestar tu presencia entre nosotros. Ya que tantas gracias concedístes a tus hijos más necesitados, con confianza de hijos te pedimos que nos des a imitar tus virtudes cristianas y ejemplos de santidad para conseguir fácilmente cuanto te hemos pedido, y como si ya lo hubiensemos conseguido, te damos gracias por tu poderosa intercesión y bondad, pues nunca has defraudado a los que con piedad se han puesto bajo tu maternal protección.

En el nombre de Dios todo poderoso.

Amén

HC9-301S 7 45720 80443 8 PRINTED IN ITALY

Our Lady of Knock Apparitions Ireland

It was August 21, 1879 and it was a rainy night. From between 7pm-9:30pm 15 people reported to have seen The Virgin Mary, St.Joseph and St. John the Evangelist appear along the side of a parish church. It was a dark night but they lit up like noonday sun. Almost all the witnesses said Mother Mary was looking up in the sky with a white cloak and a golden crown. St. Joseph stood to her right. St. John was on her left with a book in his hand as though he was teaching and with a mitre on his head. The rain was pouring down but it appeared dry where the apparitions appeared. The apparitions were 2 feet off the ground. The witnesses were thanking God for the apparition, some shed tears, it was something miraculous. Because of the witnesses, the commission found them to be trustworthy and true. There was a Novena added in 1977 that brings together millions of pilgrims every year. In 1979 Pope John Paul II came to visit the cathedral.

Prayer to Our Lady of Knock

Our Lady of Knock, Queen of Ireland, you gave hope to our people in a time of distress and comforted them in sorrow. You have inspired countless pilgrims to pray with confidence to your divine Son, remembering His promise: "Ask and you shall receive, Seek and you shall find".

Help me to remember that we are all pilgrims on the road to heaven. Fill me with love and concern for my brothers and sisters in Christ, especially those who live with me. Comfort me when I am sick or lonely or depressed. Teach me how to take part ever more reverently in the holy Mass. Pray for me now, and at the hour of my death.

Amen.

Our Lady of Pontmain, France

Our Lady of Pontmain is also referred to Our Lady of Hope. She appeared in France on January 17, 1871. It was in the middle of a Franco-Prussian war that the Virgin appeared and stopped advances to the city of Laval in France. Already the Prussians had advanced to 2/3 of France. It was Eugene, a young boy from Pontmain, that looked outside his window and saw the apparition in the sky smiling at him, a beautiful lady wearing a blue gown with golden stars and a black veil with a golden crown. The adults couldn't see her but another young boy Joseph and two young girls, described her the same way. The villagers gathered as quickly word spread about the apparition. It lasted 3 hours and the villagers said the rosary and sang songs, there was a banner beneath her that said to pray that God listens to our prayers. The same evening the Prussian army stopped their advances due to the General receiving order from his Commander. It was a miracle.

PRIÈRE À NOTRE-DAME DE PONTMAIN

Très douce Vierge Marie, tu as, dans ton apparition à Pontmain, rappelé l'importance de la prière, fortifié en nos cœurs l'Espérance et apporté la Paix.

Daigne accueillir favorablement aujourd'hui, la prière ardente que nous t'adressons pour que s'établisse dans nos cœurs, nos familles, notre Nation et toutes les Nations, la Paix, fruit de la Justice, de la Vérité, de la Charité.

Augmente en nos âmes le désir de vivre pleinement notre Foi, sans aucune compromission, dans toutes les circonstances de notre vie. Aide-nous à toujours comprendre les autres, et à les aimer profondément en Dieu. Amen.

CB 1128 – Notre-Dame de Pontmain

© Cliché : Propriété du Sanctuaire de Pontmain

21150 Flavigny-sur-Ozerain - France - www.traditions-monastiques.com/cb

Our Lady of Miraculous Medals, France

The Miraculous Medal also has the name the Medal of our Lady of Graces. It was Sister Catherine Laboure that heard the voice of a child leading her to the Virgin Mary to tell her that God was giving her a mission and not to fear and to tell everything to her spiritual director. This happened on July 19, 1830. Then on the 27 of November 1830 Mother Mary appeared to her again on the rue du Bac in Paris, France. She appeared on an oval frame standing on to of a globe, light was shining on the globe. It read O Mary conceived without original sin pray for us who have recourse in thee. She showed images of a cross and the letter M underneath it and the Sacred Heart. The Virgin Mary then asked Sister Catherine to take those images to her father confessor and that they should be put on medallions saying "All who wear them will receive great graces." It was the goldsmith Adrien Vachette who designed and produced it. Sister Catherine is now a Saint.

OUR LADY OF THE
MIRACULOUS
MEDAL
"I feel so happy
to be able to help
the children who beg
me for protection.
But so many do not
ever come to me."
O MOST HOLY VIRGIN,
O my Mother, look on my
soul with mercy, obtain for
me a spirit of prayer that
leads me always to have
recourse to thee. Obtain for
me the graces that I implore
of thee and, above all, inspire
me to pray for the graces that
thou most wants to grant me.
AMEN.
@junevreyes

Our Lady of Fatima, Portugal

This story is famous, it was May 13, 1917 and 3 children were tending to the sheep in Fatima, Portugal when they encountered the Virgin Mary. The 3 children were Lucia dos Santos, and her cousins Jacinto and Francisco Marto. Mother Mary asked them to say the rosary everyday and to meet them at the same location June 13th. She again told the children to pray the Holy Rosarys everyday to end Great wars. She also revealed that the cousins would be taken to heaven sooner than Lucia, and that she would live longer to spread the message. And she said for them to meet the 13th of the next month and so forth. By now the whole village knew what was happening and was in awe of the children communicating with Mother Mary. It was on October 13th, 1917 that everyone was amazed Mother Mary promised a miracle and it was the miracle of the sun. The sun was dancing, was zig-zagging in the sky, and it rained and supposedly the floor dried up quickly. The children saw Jesus, Saint Joseph and Our Lady of Sorrows blessing the crowd that came. The children had seen the Virgin a total of 6 times each and she always told them to pray the rosary for the sinners of this world and the next world. She revealed prophecies to the children which Lucia revealed to a select few. Pope John Paul 2 knew the third secret of the prophecy it was about his attempted assassination.

I have a special love for Our Lady of Fatima because of the muslim ladies in the world named Fatima remind me of her. I know its just a name but they are veiled like her and hopefully just as pure as her. She brings us Christians closer to muslims. Also a strange coincidence, when I wrote the story of Our Lady of Fatima it was on Oct. 13th, 2019, 102 years after the miracle of the sun occurred. Quite a coincidence 😊

Prayer to Our Lady of Fatima

O Most Holy Virgin Mary, Queen of the most holy Rosary, you were pleased to appear to the children of Fatima and reveal a glorious message. We implore you, inspire in our hearts a fervent love for the recitation of the Rosary. By meditating on the mysteries of the redemption that are recalled therein may we obtain the graces and virtues that we ask, through the merits of Jesus Christ, our Lord and Redeemer. *Amen.*

Share Catholic
www.ShareCatholic.com

Our Lady of Guadeloupe, Mexico

This is my favorite apparition, I pray to her every night and hope to be lucky enough to go visit where she appeared one day. Here's her story, there was a young man named Juan Diego, who is now a Saint (Dec. 9), shepherding his flock and La Virgen of Guadeloupe appeared to him from December 9th to December 12th 1531 asking him to have a shrine built where she appeared in Tepeyac Hill, Mexico. He went to the bishop and told him what happened but he said he won't have anything built without a sign. La Virgen of Guadeloupe appeared 4 times to Juan Diego and she told him the 4th time to gather a bunch of roses and his tilma and go see the bishop. When he met up with the Bishop he undid his tilma and there was roses everywhere and a beautiful image of Our Lady of Guadeloupe which is still at the shrine today. The bishop approved of this sign and built the shrine.

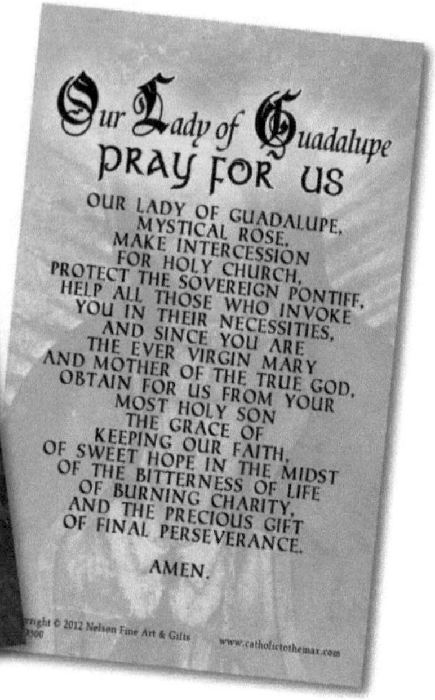
Our Lady of Guadalupe
PRAY FOR US
OUR LADY OF GUADALUPE,
MYSTICAL ROSE,
MAKE INTERCESSION
FOR HOLY CHURCH,
PROTECT THE SOVEREIGN PONTIFF,
HELP ALL THOSE WHO INVOKE
YOU IN THEIR NECESSITIES,
AND SINCE YOU ARE
THE EVER VIRGIN MARY
AND MOTHER OF THE TRUE GOD,
OBTAIN FOR US FROM YOUR
MOST HOLY SON
THE GRACE OF
KEEPING OUR FAITH,
OF SWEET HOPE IN THE MIDST
OF THE BITTERNESS OF LIFE
OF BURNING CHARITY,
AND THE PRECIOUS GIFT
OF FINAL PERSEVERANCE.
AMEN.
© 2012 Nelson Fine Art & Gifts
www.catholictothemax.com

Our Lady of Lourdes, France

On February 11th, 1858 Our Lady appeared to a 14 year old Saint Bernadette Soubirous in the cave of Massabielle in Lourdes, France. She was gathering firewood with her sister and a friend when Our

Mother spoke to her. Our lady appeared 17 times that year. A large church was built at the site and now Lourdes has become a major pilgrimage site. Lourdes has the second most hotels aside from Paris, in France. On several occasions Our Lady appeared to her in the cave, grotto. One time Our Lady told her to drink the water that was beneath her, she dug and after a lot of mud she found a clear stream. This stream attracts many worldwide today. Many have been cured of their illnesses because of it. On March 25, 1858 Our Lady told her that she was the Immaculate Conception. She described Our Lady wearing all white, with a blue sash around her waist and yellow roses on her feet, same color as the chain of her rosary and the beads were white and there was a dazzling light. The last apparition was July 16, 1858. Aside from Fatima it is the second most visited Marian sighting in the world. Almost 4-6 million people travel there every year.

Our Lady of Medugorje,

On June 24th, 1981 our blessed Lady had appeared to 6 Herzegovinians teenagers. Where formerly was known as Yugoslavia. She appeared for 7 days in a row. The 6 teenagers were Ivanka Ivanković, Mirjana Dragićević, Vicka Ivanković,Ivan Dragićević, Ivan Ivanković and Milka Pavlović. The first day they saw a lady holding a baby in her arms. They knew the lady of Mother Mary. The second day the Lady appeared again at the same sight without the baby in her arms. There was a flash of light and she appeared, indescribably beautiful. She motioned to come closer and pray and they did. The children asked for a sign so others don't think they are lying or crazy. The third day she appeared as usual at 6 oclock at night at the same sight. There was a flash of light and the children knew it was her and they prayed and she appeared beautiful as always. Mirjana asked her name and she said The Blessed Virgin Mary. The fourth day the Lady appeared again and the children asked for a sign so people didn't think they were lying or taking drugs. The blessed Virgin said "do not be afraid of anything." The fifth day there was a crowd of 15000 people waiting to see Mother Mary. Her message was for the priests that they should firmly believe so that others too will believe. On the sixth day the children prayed and the blessed Virgin appeared. An atheist doctor asked the children if he can touch our lady and they guided him to her shoulder and he felt a tingling sensation and sensed there was something there. Another brought their child there to be healed and he miraculously did. The crowds were getting bigger. On the last day they were 1 kilometre away from the site in Podbrdo, they prayed to Mother Mary and she appeared. She appeared to the children in many different occasions afterwards and when they prayed. She appeared until January 15, 1982. But Mirjana still claims to see Our Mother Mary and reports what she says and her warnings on youtube and on websites. Here's one of Mirjana's websites:

https://www.medjugorje.ws/

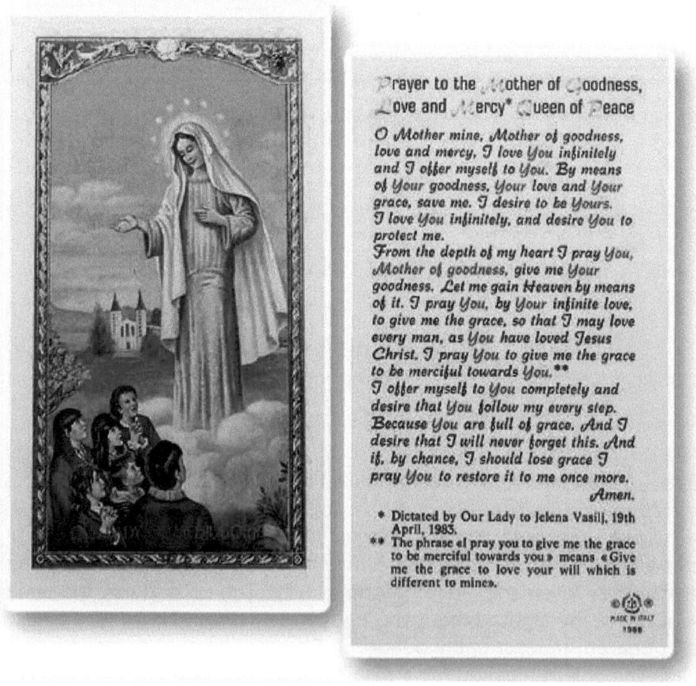

Our Lady of Akita, Japan

On July 6th, 1973 Our Lady appeared to Sister Agnes Katsuko Sasagawa in the outskirt of Akita, Japan. She gave her messages of prayer and reciting the Rosary the three times she saw Our Lady. Before she appeared to her the first time she received a cross on her left palm, like a stigmata. Sister Sagagawa had visions of her guardian angel. And the guardian angel told her that Mother Mary's pain is more than hers with the stigmata. The angel then guided her to the chapel and there was a light that shone from the wooden carved statue of Mother Mary. Sister Sasagawa is deaf but she heard Mother Mary speak and tell her that she will be cured form her deafness. Mother Mary asked to pray for the bishops, Pope and priests. The statue is known to weep real tears. It was broadcasted on live tv. About 101 times it has occurred. Also Sister Sasagawa was cured from her deafness after the apparitions.

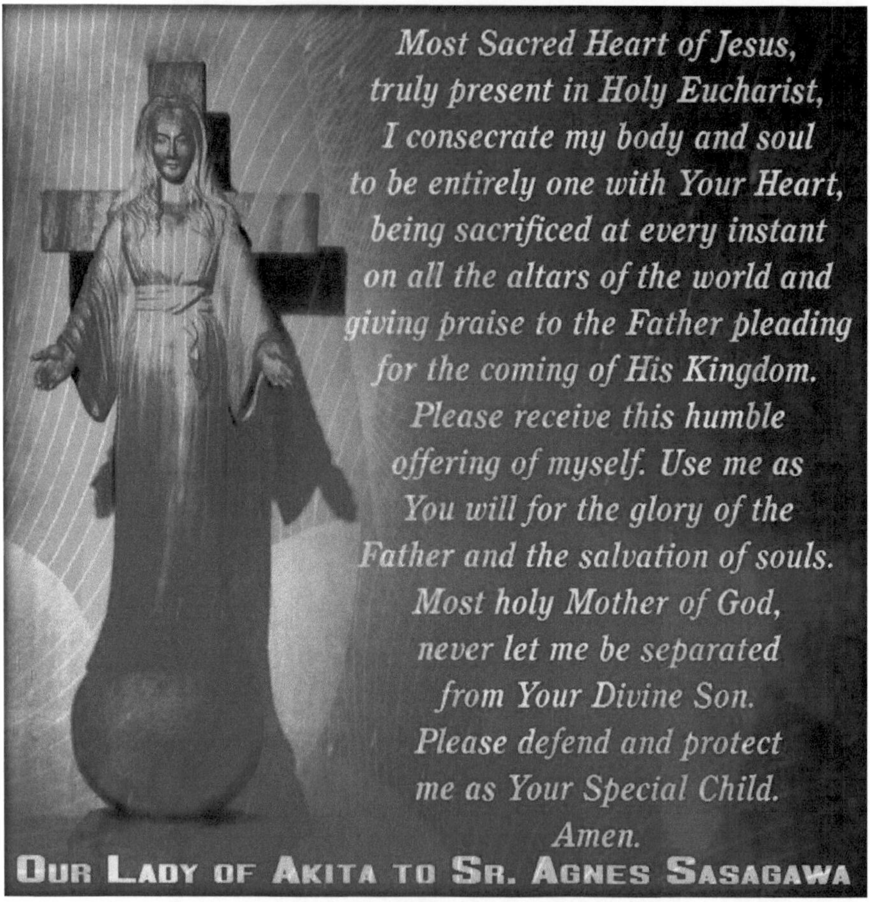

Virgin of the Poor, Belgium

She is also known as Our Lady of the Poor. Between January and March 1933, Our Lady appeared to Mariette Beco, a twelve year old girl, in the province of Liege, Banneaux, Belgium. Our Lady declared that she was the Virgin of the Poor and she wore a white robe with a blue sash around her waist and a transparent veil. January 16th, 1933 was the first apparition. Mariette was looking outside her kitchen window and she saw our Lady there in the garden calling out to her. Her mother didn't want her to go but she went. She appeared 8 times after that the last on March 2nd, 1933. One of her visions with Our Lady she was asked to plunge her hands in a spring which had miraculous qualities and healed illnesses. Still today many pilgrims go to the spring for its miracles. Many made fun of Mariette and her visions but she kept on. Our Lady asked for a chapel to be built, and it was built. Mariette led a quiet life, got married and died December 2, 2011 at 90 years old.

Our Lady of Banneux, Belgium

Our Lady of Gietrzald, Poland

On June 27 1877 our Lady appeared for the first time to Justyna Szafrynska and then she appeared to another girl Barbara Samulowska too. She was shining bright and the girls asked her who she was and she answered, "I am the Blessed Virgin Mary the Immaculate Conception." They asked her what she wants from them and she said to them to pray the rosary daily. The girls asked if they brought the sick would they be healed and Mother Mary said that the sick will be healed but they need to pray the rosary. She encouraged us to pray zealously. Mother Mary has blessed a spring that was there and many healings have occurred and lots of pilgrim go every year. Her last apparition was September 16, 1877 where Mother Mary blessed many people and told them to pray zealously.

Our Lady of Gaietrzwałd

First Apparition: June 27, 1877
Gietrzwałd, Poland
Feast Day: September 8

Traditional prayer

Mother of our Lord, healer of human souls and bodies, Lady of Giettrzwald, You who blessed this place with your presence, please turn your loving eyes toward me and ask Your Son Jesus Christ for the favors I am in need of *(mention request)*. Compassionate and merciful Virgin Mother, I am forever Yours. Amen.

Hymn to the Blessed Virgin Mary of Gietrzwałd

(by Andrzej Samulowski)

It was just the sunset,
When the wonderful brilliant star
Arose in the Warmian land
To shed light with its rays.
This news almost by a miracle
Was spread among the people,
Far and near, they would say:
In Warmia, there are new miracles.

Copyright © 2018, Traditio Designs, LLC
www.traditiocatholica.com

Our Lady of Czestochowa, Poland

Also known as the Black Madonna, and her feast day is on August 26. On September 15, 1920 Our Lady appeared after the Polish soldiers were praying fervently to her. She appeared on the clouds above River Vistula above Warsaw and the Russians were defeated and they called that miracle "the Miracle of Vistula". There was another time that Our Lady listened to the Pole's prayers. In 1655 the Swedish army wanted to invade Czestochowa and after the Polish soldiers prayed fervently the enemy retreated.

Prayer to Our Lady of Czestochowa

(To be said each day)

Holy Mother of Czestochowa, Thou art full of grace, goodness and mercy.

I consecrate to Thee all my thoughts, words and actions- my soul and body.

I beseech Thy blessings and especially prayers for my salvation.

Today, I consecrate myself to Thee, Good Mother, totally- with body and soul amid joy and sufferings to obtain for myself and others Thy blessings on this earth and eternal life in Heaven.

Amen.

® HC9-405E 7 45720 05476 5 PRINTED IN ITALY

Our Lady of Lezajsk, Poland

In 1578, there was once a pious woodcutter named Thomas Michalek. He was in the forest and he saw a bright light and it was Our Lady. She told him, "Thomas I chose this place. Here my son will be loved and respected and whosoever shall call upon my intercession, will receive my blessing." She asked him to go to the authorities to built a church where she was. Thomas was scared and did nothing. She again appeared to him and urged him to go to the authorities to build a church there. This time he did what he was told but they didn't believe him. The curate even brought Thomas to court. When that curate died, the new parish priest built the church, yay!

MIRACULOUS IMAGE OF OUR LADY
OF CONSOLATION IN LEZAJSK
O Glorious Lady of Lezajsk,
To you we render our humble thanks that in union with
St Joseph, Your Bridegroom,
You have sanctified this place with Your gentle touch and
remain here in the sign of Your miraculous image, to be
with us in all the affairs of our daily life.
O Mother of Consolation help us to defend the dignity of
every human person, their life and love, within ourselves
and within our families.
O Gracious Mother, support us in fulfilling our mission
in this modern world, be for us The Star of Consolation,
The Smile of Forgiveness, and The Sun of Hope that leads
to everlasting Joy.
O Mother we implore You to intercede for us with Your
Son, to who You are also Mother. Amen
PICCOLLAGE

Our Lady of Siluva, Lithuania

In the summer of 1608 there were children tending sheep in Siluva, Lithuania and there appeared a beautiful woman holding a baby in her arms. They went to go get the adults and when they arrived at the same location she was crying and told them that she wanted a church built again in the same place she was. There used to be a Catholic church there before. A wooden church was built but then it was too small for the amount of pilgrims that came to visit so they built a bigger church. The church is now called the Basilic of the Nativity of Mary.

APPARITION OF OUR LADY
AT SILUVA, LITHUANIA,
1608

MALDA

Į APSIREIŠKUSIĄ DIEVO MOTINĄ

Švenčiausioji Mergelė Marija, kuri Šiluvos laukuose pasirodei piemenėliams, kuri skausmo ašaromis laistei akmenį, išlikusį altoriaus vietoje, ir skundo balsu kalbėjai: "Čia kitados buvo garbinamas mano sūnus, o dabar ariama ir sėjama!" Duok, kad Tavo ašarų sugraudinti, mes, kaip kitados mūsų protėviai, keltume Tavo Sūnaus garbę apleistoje mūsų širdžių dirvoje, atstatytume griūvančias mūsų šeimų šventoves, permaldautume Viešpatį už visos mūsų tautos apsileidimus ir nuodėmes.

O Dievo Motina, mes trokštam iškelti iš užmaršties griūvėsių Tavo apsireiškimo garbę, dar labiau garbinti Tave, mūsų žemės Globėja ir Tau padedant išmelsti mūsų kraštui gyvą tikėjimo dvasią. Per Kristų mūsų Viešpatį. Amen.

(Iš Kun. St. Ylos "Šv. Marija")

(Cum Approbatione Ecclesiastica)

Our Lady of La Salette, France

On September 19th, 1846 Our Lady appeared weeping to two children Maximin Giraud and Melanie Calvat in La Salette, Fallavaux, France. Our lady was dressed in a white robe with pearls and a gold apron, with roses at her feet and white shoes. She had a crucifix around her neck suspended from a chain. She spoke to the children through the tears telling them to tell the tell everyone to keep the 7th day holy and not to use God's name in vain or else there will be a famine. The people didn't listen and there was famine in the winter of 1946-1947 in the areas of Europe especially France and Ireland. Then our Lady's apparition vanished to the hills weeping. There is a basilica and a shrine in her honor in France.

Memorare to Our Lady of La Salette

Remember, Our Lady of La Salette, true Mother of Sorrows, the tears you shed for us on Calvary. Remember also the care you have taken to keep us faithful to Christ, your Son. Having done so much for your children, you will not now abandon us. Comforted by this consoling thought, we come to you pleading, despite our infidelities and ingratitude. Virgin of Reconciliation, do not reject our prayers, but intercede for us, obtain for us the grace to love Jesus above all else. May we console you by living a holy life and so come to share the eternal life Christ gained by his cross. Amen.

La Salette Invocation

Our Lady of La Salette, Reconciler of sinners, pray without ceasing for us who have recourse to you.

KE24-294 Kilgarlin

Our Lady of Zeitoun, Egypt

Our Lady of Zeitoun appeared numerus times, sometimes for short periods other times for hours, starting April 2, 1968 to May 4, 1968. Her appearance led to many miracles, first the conversion of sinners into the faith and second in the number of healings that occurred that couldn't be explained by physicians. They say that the Virgin Mary Coptic Orthodox Church in Cairo Egypt is where the Holy Family stayed when they fled from Bethlehem and now Mother Mary was reappearing to give hope to all her Middle Eastern children.

Holy Mother of Light

Holy Mother of Light, Spouse of the Holy Ghost, O sweet and gentle Lady, Immaculate Mother of God, I choose thee this day to be the Mistress and Lady of my home. Guard it, dear Mother, from pestilence, fire, lightning, inundation. and tempest; from schism and heresy; from the depredations of burglars and the malice of our enemies. Protect its inmates, sweet Mary, watch their going out and their coming in, preserve them from sudden and unprovided death. Keep us from all sin and harm, and pray for us to God, that we may live in His service, and depart from this life in His grace. Amen.

Our Lady of Beauraing, Belgium

Also known as Our Lady of the Golden Heart. Her feast day is on November 29th. It was on that day back in 1932 that she appeared to 5 children, Fernande, Gilberte, Albert, Andree and Gilberte. She was in a white robe and she identified herself to the children as the Immaculate Virgin and showed her golden heart. She appeared to the children 32 more times afterwards, her last appearance the 3 of January 1933, and she asked the children to pray, pray and pray and to have a chapel built where she appeared for pilgrims. Many cures have occurred at the site where she appeared. All 5 children grew up, married and lived quiet lives.

Our Lady of Laus, France

Bob and Penny Lord

Benoite (Benedicta) Rencurel was the lady Mother Mary appeared to. She was a shepherdess whose father had died when she was young. The first apparition was on May 1664 and she continued appearing to her throughout her life until she died in 1718. During the apparitions Mother Mary asked to pray for sinners and she asked to build a church and a house for priests to bring more people to confessions, conversions and penance. The holy site draws 120000 pilgrims and many miracles have occurred there especially when oil from a lamp is put on a wound. Benedicta received the stigmata during her lifetime and is venerable and waiting to become a saint.

- ## Prayer of the Laus

Lord,

Full of tenderness and mercy,

you are blessed in your Son Jesus

who has given us Laus, refuge of sinners.

You are blessed in Mary,

our Mother, who comes to this refuge to visit her people in their suffering.

You are blessed in Benoîte Rencurel, for her testimony,

and for the 54 years she spent listening to the Beautiful Lady.

Therefore, Lord, through the intercession of Mary,

dwelling place of the Holy Spirit,

change our hearts of stone into hearts of flesh.

Grant that, following Benoîte,

we will let ourselves be transformed so as to live today and tomorrow faithful to the Gospel, in the Church and in the world.

Amen.

Our Lady of Mount Carmel

On July 16th 1251, the Virgin Mary appeared to Saint Simon Stock (May 16th) with a scapular in her hand saying to him "Take, beloved son, this scapular of the order as a badge of my confraternity and for you and all Carmelites a special sign of grace; whoever dies in this garment, will not suffer everlasting fire. It is the sign of salvation, a safeguard in dangers, a pledge of peace and of the covenant". He soon after instituted the confraternity called the Brown Scapulars. Her feast day is on July 16th.

Our Lady of Kibeho, Rwanda

Our Lady of Kibeho's feast day is Novemeber 28th, to commemorate her first apparition to Alphonsine Mumureke in 1981. She appeared to two other teenage girls from a small town called Kibeho, in southwestern Rwanda. The two other girls were Nathalie Mukamazimpaka and Marie Claire Mukangango. She appeared to them in the course of the 1980s. On August 19, 1982 they all saw a vision of violence, dismemberment and destruction. Mother of the Word, as she was called, was warning about the genocide that occurred a few years later in Rwanda between the tribes Tutsi and Hutu. The Virgin told Marie Claire Mukangango to pray the Chaplet of seven Sorrows to obtain favors of repentance. A Marian Shrine was built in Kibeho to honor Our Lady's apparitions.

OUR LADY OF KIBEHO

The Blessed Virgin Mary appeared to 3 teenagers in Kibeho, Rwanda in 1981, as Our Lady of Kibeho. On August 19, 1982, those who saw the visions reported gruesome sights (rivers of blood, sliced heads, etc.) which some today regard as an ominous foreshadowing of the Rwandan Genocide of 1994, and particularly in that specific location in 1995. Catholic Bishop Augustin Misago approved public devotion linked to the apparitions on 15th August 1988 and declared their authenticity on 29th June 2001.

facebook.com/catholicpriest-alterchristusofficialpage

Our Lady of Lavang, Vietnam

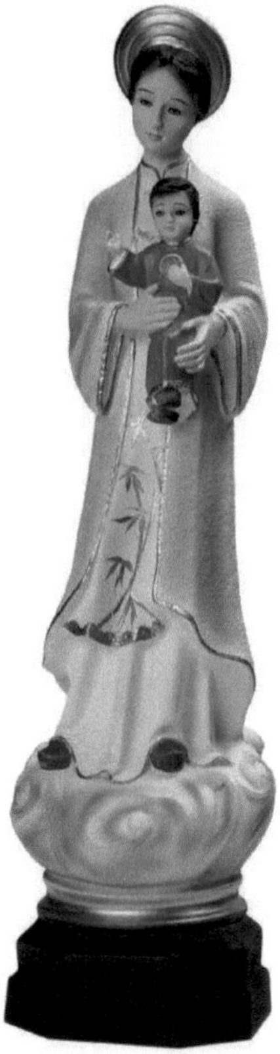

In 1798 Mother Mary appeared to a group of Vietnam Catholics that escaped to the jungle to escape persecution. They escaped in 1785 and they lived there many years and prayed the rosary every day but the water was contaminated where they were. Mother Mary said take the leaves of this plant and make a tea and they were cured from their illnesses. They heard not long after the apparition that the persecution ended. Most returned to their homes and spoke about the apparition and word spread. Even the Buddhists believed. A basilica was built in the honor of Our Lady of Lavang.

OUR LADY OF LAVANG

PRAY FOR US!

Blessed Lady of
Lavang be my mother
and comfort me,
especially in times of
trial and unhappiness.
Enter my heart and
stay with me wherever
I may go. Grant that
one day, through you,
I may find rest and
peace in my Father's
house.
Amen.

Buy your books fast and straightforward online - at one of world's fastest growing online book stores! Environmentally sound due to Print-on-Demand technologies.

Buy your books online at

www.morebooks.shop

Kaufen Sie Ihre Bücher schnell und unkompliziert online – auf einer der am schnellsten wachsenden Buchhandelsplattformen weltweit! Dank Print-On-Demand umwelt- und ressourcenschonend produzi ert.

Bücher schneller online kaufen

www.morebooks.shop

KS OmniScriptum Publishing
Brivibas gatve 197
LV-1039 Riga, Latvia
Telefax: +371 686 204 55

info@omniscriptum.com
www.omniscriptum.com

OMNIScriptum

MIX
Papier aus verantwortungsvollen Quellen
Paper from responsible sources
FSC® C105338

Printed by Books on Demand GmbH, Norderstedt / Germany